Please return or renew this item by the last date shown.
You may renew items (unless they have been requested
by another customer) by telephoning, writing to or calling
in at any library.  100% recycled paper   *BKS 1 (5/95)*

A
SAMURAI
CASTLE

Series Editor	David Salariya
Book Editor	Jenny Millington

Author:
Fiona Macdonald studied history at Cambridge University and at the University of East Anglia, where she is a part-time tutor. She has written many books for children on historical topics, including *A Roman Fort* and *A 16th-Century Mosque* in this series.

Illustrators:
David Antram was born in Brighton in 1958. He studied at Eastbourne College of Art and then worked in advertising for fifteen years. He lives in Sussex with his wife and two children.

John James was born in London in 1959. He studied at Eastbourne College of Art and has specialized in historical reconstruction since leaving art school in 1982. He lives in Sussex with his wife and children.

David Antram pp. 6–7, pp. 8–9, pp.16–17, pp.18–19, pp. 22–23, pp. 24–25, pp. 32–33, pp. 34–35, pp. 42–43; **John James** pp. 10–11, pp. 12–13, pp. 14–15, pp. 20–21, pp. 26–27, pp. 28–29, pp. 30–31, pp. 36–37, pp. 38–39, pp. 40–41.

Consultant:
Helena Gomm studied English Literature at Oxford University. She lived in Japan for five years, where she taught English. She now lives and works in London.

Created, designed and produced by
The Salariya Book Co Ltd, Brighton, UK

First published in 1995
by Macdonald Young Books

Macdonald Young Books Ltd
Campus 400
Maylands Avenue
Hemel Hempstead
Herts
HP2 7EZ

© The Salariya Book Co Ltd MCMXCV

ISBN 0-7500-1586-1

A catalogue record for this book is available from the British Library.

Printed and bound in Portugal by Edições ASA

A SAMURAI CASTLE

FIONA MACDONALD

DAVID ANTRAM

JOHN JAMES

MACDONALD YOUNG BOOKS

CONTENTS

掠疾
如如
山風

INTRODUCTION

If you were a time-traveller, visiting Japan at any moment during the past 400 years, you could hardly fail to be impressed by the magnificent castles you would see. These castles were mostly built during the 16th and 17th centuries, for samurai (warrior) families. During that time, many castles were erected, and thousands of skilled workers were employed to construct them. Why were these castles built? How were they made without modern cranes, bulldozers and earth-moving machinery? Who paid for them, and where did the money come from? What was it like to live, work, fight and sometimes die within their walls? You can find the answers to these questions – and many others – in this book.

Only a few samurai castles survive today. Their carefully-preserved remains can tell us a great deal about building methods and construction details. But we can find out more – about the thoughts, feelings and behaviour of the people who built them – from contemporary documents giving detailed descriptions of samurai warriors and their lifestyle, and from Japanese pictures painted on scrolls and beautiful folding screens.

WHO WERE THE SAMURAI?

In 1592, samurai warriors led 200,000 Japanese soldiers to invade Korea. At first they were successful, but were soon forced to retreat when the mighty Chinese empire came to Korea's aid.

Samurai were warriors and landowners, who lived in Japan. From the 12th to the 18th centuries, they were the most powerful group of people in the country. Why was this?

Samurai were rich, because they had land. It was farmed by peasants who grew rice to give to the samurai as rent. Rice was the chief form of wealth in Japan. Samurai had weapons – the samurai badge of rank was a daisho, or matching pair of swords. Even samurai women wore a dagger tucked into the wide silk sashes around their waists.

Above all, samurai had private armies, which gave them the power to do what they liked – as long as rival samurai did not try to stop them. Samurai admired, feared and respected one another, but the only man they obeyed was the shogun, the national army commander-in-chief.

However, samurai were more than just fighters. They were members of a ruling class who prided themselves on their ancestry, bravery and sense of honour, as well as on their fighting skills. Samurai were born, not made. To be a real samurai, you had to have samurai parents; occasionally, a man might be adopted into a samurai family, but only if he had shown himself worthy of such a noble reward.

The samurai Minamoto Yoritomo (1147–98) was a great warlord. By 1185, after five years of fighting, Yoritomo won control of most of Japan. Recognising his power, the Japanese emperor made him 'Sei-i Tai Shogun' (Great General Subduing the Barbarians).

Officially, Yoritomo was leader of all the emperor's warriors, with a special duty to defend Japan from invaders. But, in fact, he was more powerful even than that. For the next 700 years, shoguns, not emperors, were the real rulers of Japan.

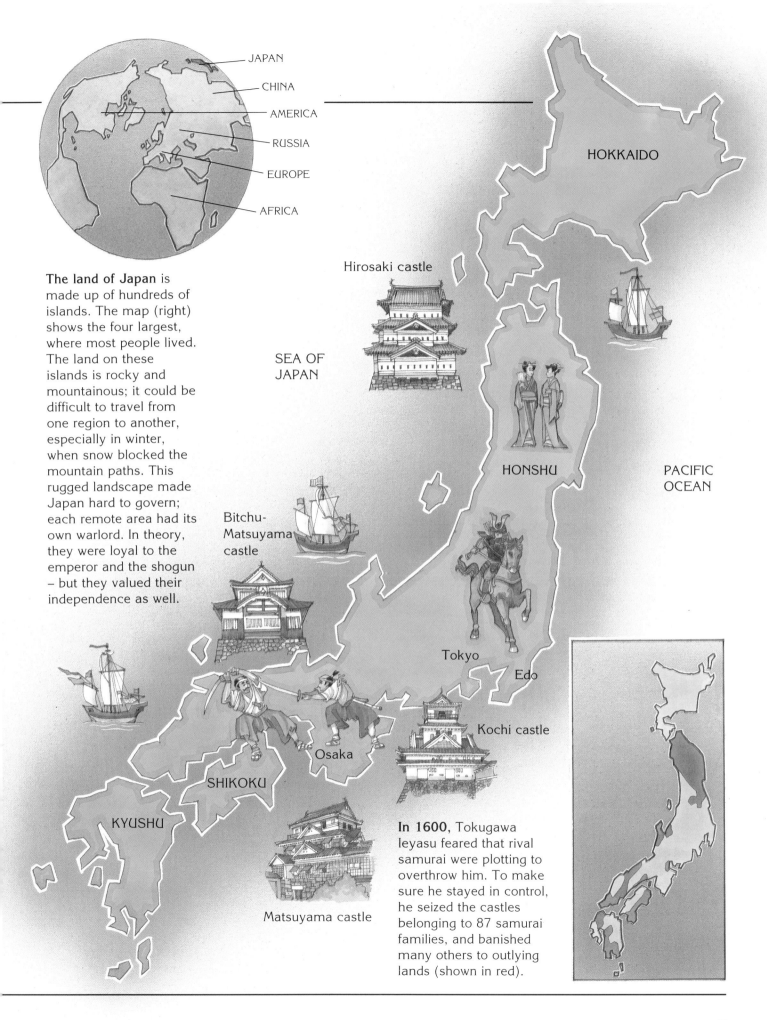

JAPAN
CHINA
AMERICA
RUSSIA
EUROPE
AFRICA

The land of Japan is made up of hundreds of islands. The map (right) shows the four largest, where most people lived. The land on these islands is rocky and mountainous; it could be difficult to travel from one region to another, especially in winter, when snow blocked the mountain paths. This rugged landscape made Japan hard to govern; each remote area had its own warlord. In theory, they were loyal to the emperor and the shogun – but they valued their independence as well.

Hirosaki castle

SEA OF JAPAN

HOKKAIDO

HONSHU

PACIFIC OCEAN

Bitchu-Matsuyama castle

Tokyo

Edo

Kochi castle

Osaka

SHIKOKU

KYUSHU

Matsuyama castle

In 1600, Tokugawa Ieyasu feared that rival samurai were plotting to overthrow him. To make sure he stayed in control, he seized the castles belonging to 87 samurai families, and banished many others to outlying lands (shown in red).

JAPANESE SOCIETY

Although samurai were the most powerful group in Japan, they were not the most high-ranking. The emperor was at the top of society, refined, remote and god-like, and believed to be descended from the sun. The shogun, who ruled for the emperor, came next in rank. Originally, shoguns had been chosen for their skill as war-leaders. But after 1603, all shoguns came from one ruling dynasty, founded by the shogun Tokugawa Ieyasu, who lived from 1542 to 1616. By defeating any samurai who dared oppose him, he brought peace to Japan after years of civil war. Samurai had the next highest status, but they were not all equal.

In the towns, merchants and traders produced luxury goods – such as fine clothes and ivory carvings – for rich samurai to buy. Actors, dancers and musicians provided entertainment.

Japanese society:
(1) Buddhist priest.
(2) Buddhist monk.
(3) Buddhist nun.
(4) Actors. (5) Town traders. (6) Country craftsmen.
(7) Farmer.

(8) Low-ranking soldiers in a samurai's private army (called ashigaru).
(9) High-ranking samurai (called daimyo).
(10) The shogun, leading warlord and ruler of all Japan.

The emperor's court:
(A) Useful people: servants, cooks, cleaners, maids.
(B) Scribes, clerks and officials, (C) Old noble families, some holding ancient honorary posts.
(D) The emperor.

A

B

C

D

From 794, the emperor and his court lived in the ancient capital city of Kyoto. There they led an elegant life, following ancient traditions, but had no political power. That was based at the shogun's castle, and, after 1603, at the shogun's new capital city of Edo (present-day Tokyo).

Top samurai, called 'daimyo' (lords), owned great estates and fine castles. There were also lower-class samurai, who fought as officers in daimyo private armies. Next in rank came ordinary soldiers, or 'ashigaru'.

The peasants who farmed the daimyo's estates were often very poor. But they ranked next after the samurai and ashigaru, because they produced rice to feed everyone else in Japan. Buddhist priests, monks and nuns might be respected, but only if they came from families of samurai rank. Craft-workers and merchants were at the bottom of the social scale.

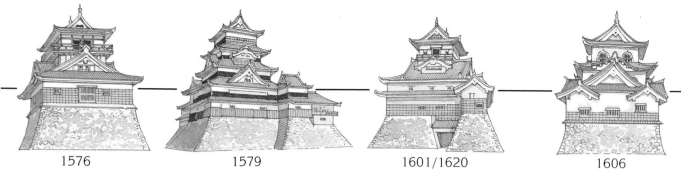

1576   1579   1601/1620   1606

CHOOSING THE SITE

Why did samurai build castles? First and foremost, for defence. The earliest castle builders chose naturally well-protected sites – mountain crags or rocky cliffs. The first forts and castles were simple and small, just strong stone walls around a central keep (or 'tenshu') where warlords and their soldiers could take refuge.

Later, after Yoritomo became shogun in 1185, he needed help to rule the country. He recruited loyal samurai, made them daimyo, and gave them land. To administer their new estates and to display their proud new status, these top-rank samurai built splendid castles throughout Japan. The new castles were much bigger than the old stone forts. More space was needed now, to house the daimyo's family in comfort, and to accommodate their soldiers, servants and officials. New castle sites were chosen, too. Some were still in the mountains, others were in lowland valleys or on coastal plains. There, castles could guard the roads and rivers connecting daimyo territories with hostile neighbouring lands, where enemy samurai patrolled. Many new sites lacked strong natural defences, but artificial barriers could quickly be built.

Before the strong central keep (called a 'tenshu') of a castle could be built, its outer defences had to be planned. This was the task of well-trained professional architects. In mountainous areas, or on steep river banks, loose rocks and slippery slopes formed natural barriers against attack.

On lowland castle sites, high, steep banks of earth were heaped up, deep moats were dug, and strong outer walls were constructed. Foundations were laid, on which gatehouses and tall watchtowers could be built, where samurai soldiers could keep guard.

Most samurai castles have disappeared. Shown above are 8 of the surviving ones with the dates when they were built:
(1) Maruoka.
(2) Matsumoto.
(3) Inuyama.
(4) Hikone. (5) Himeji.
(6) Matsue.
(7) Marugame.
(8) Uwajima.

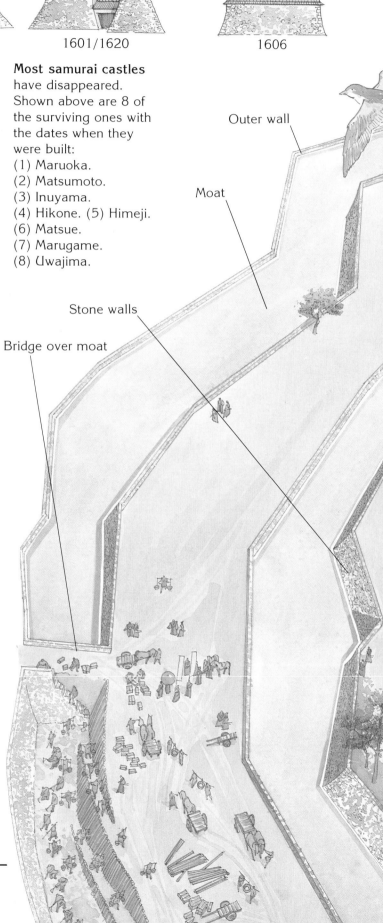

Outer wall

Moat

Stone walls

Bridge over moat

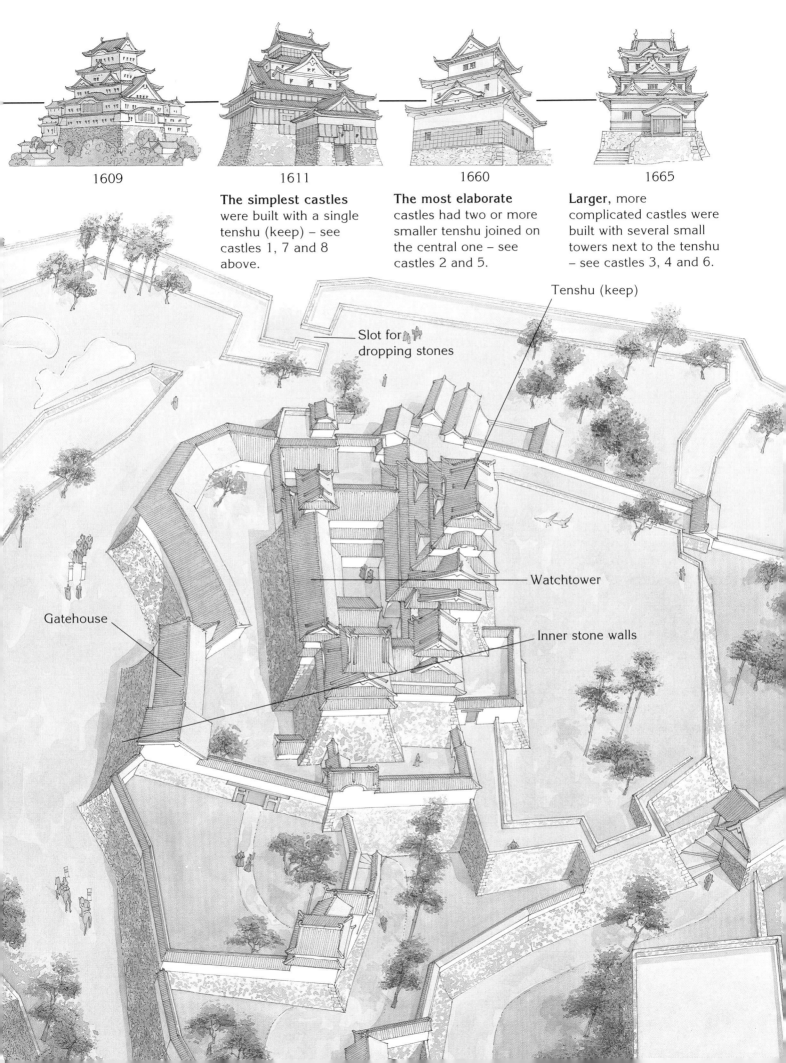

1609

1611

1660

1665

The simplest castles were built with a single tenshu (keep) – see castles 1, 7 and 8 above.

The most elaborate castles had two or more smaller tenshu joined on the central one – see castles 2 and 5.

Larger, more complicated castles were built with several small towers next to the tenshu – see castles 3, 4 and 6.

Tenshu (keep)

Slot for dropping stones

Watchtower

Gatehouse

Inner stone walls

BUILDING THE CASTLE

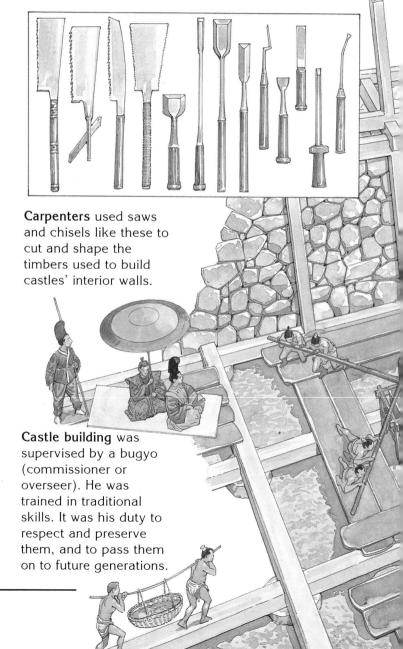

'Disordered piling' was made of small stones packed tightly together, leaving no cracks for attackers to find footholds and climb up.

'Burdock piling' was made of large, carefully-shaped blocks fitted together over a mound of earth. Cracks were filled with pebbles.

Castle walls were built without mortar to join stones together, so each stone could move slightly without the whole building cracking.

Many walls were built with a curved profile, rather than a straight edge. This also increased their stability during an earthquake.

Samurai castles were built by hand. The huge boulders used to construct walls had to be rough-hewn at quarries or collected from mountainsides, then sorted, lifted and fitted together without the help of power-driven machines. They also had to be carried to castle building sites. In many areas, paths were too steep to use wheeled carts, so everything had to be carried in baskets slung from poles.

Enormous quantities of stone were used: the three walls encircling Himeji Castle (built 1609) have a surface area of over 100,000 square metres. Understandably, walls were usually left rough. But a few castles have stonework chiselled to a superfine finish, as smooth as cloth. Inside the stone walls, castle buildings were made of wood and plaster. The strong timber framework was prefabricated at a master carpenter's workshop, then assembled at the castle site. The standard of woodwork was very high, with precision joints and intricately-carved doors, window frames and rafters. Stonemasons and carpenters were very well trained, and were proud of their traditional skills. Boys were apprenticed to a master craftsman at 13, and spent many years learning their craft.

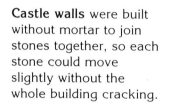

Carpenters used saws and chisels like these to cut and shape the timbers used to build castles' interior walls.

Castle building was supervised by a bugyo (commissioner or overseer). He was trained in traditional skills. It was his duty to respect and preserve them, and to pass them on to future generations.

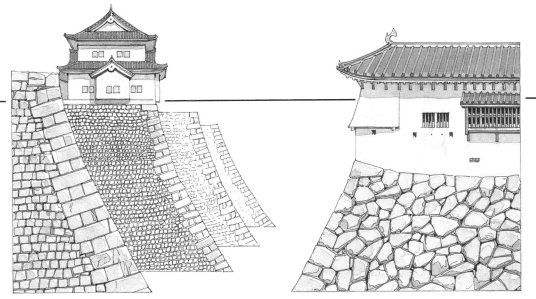

Instructions for making a roof, 1658 (above).

Walls were covered with wood strips, hemp and plaster (below).

Builders took special care with the corner-stones of walls. They were wedged together in an interlocking pattern, for extra strength.

Walls with zig-zag corners were extra-strong, and also very decorative. Japanese builders called them 'folding fans'.

Top samurai asked for their castle walls to be built curving upwards. This was a sign of wealth and status. It was also thought to look good.

CASTLE DESIGN

The period 1570-1690 is often called the 'Golden Age' of Japanese castle building. What made these castles so special? Partly, their size. Unlike traditional Japanese buildings, they were several storeys high. For example, Matsumoto castle (completed 1596) had floors on six levels in its keep. 'Golden Age' castles were also admired for their innovative layout. They were planned as clusters of towers, and included features – gateways, courtyards, reception halls – borrowed from all kinds of traditional buildings, from temples to townhouses.

The resulting castles were very beautiful, with carved and painted woodwork and steep, soaring roofs. The outer walls of Matsue castle (completed 1611) were covered in shiny black lacquer (varnish), earning it the nickname 'Raven Castle'. Hikone castle (completed 1603) was decorated in gold. Himeji castle (completed 1609) was covered in special, fireproof white plaster. This, plus its graceful, curving gables, won it the name 'White Egret Castle'. Until the early 17th century, these magnificent castles had an extra purpose: to threaten the shogun by displaying samurai power. That is why, in 1615, shogun Ieyasu banned samurai from building more than one castle on each of their estates.

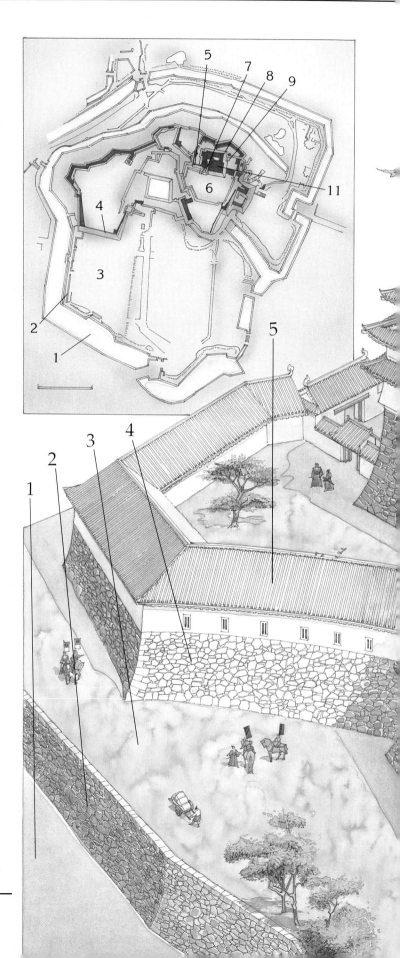

Shown here is Himeji castle, built in 1609. The small picture on this page shows a plan of the castle.

(1) Moat.
(2) Outer walls.
(3) Outer bailey.
(4) Inner walls.
(5) Kitchens, stables, workshops, rest rooms for soldiers.
(6) Inner bailey.
(7) Watchtower.
(8) Side tower.
(9) Minor gate house.
(10) Fortified passage linking side tower with keep.
(11) Main keep containing: main hall for receiving visitors; offices for daimyo's administrative staff; watchtower and gun storage room; kitchens and food stores; daimyo's living rooms; soldier's rooms.
(12) Impressive roof.
(13) Fine plastered walls.

12

13

11

10

7

8

6

9

ELEGANT INTERIORS

Traditionally, Japanese houses did not have solid inside walls dividing one room from another. Instead, the inner space was partitioned by wood and paper screens, which could be moved as required to create areas for living, sleeping or eating.

The space inside a castle was arranged in much the same way. Originally, strength and security were considered by samurai to be more important than elegance or fine design. But soon, castle interiors began to be planned – at least in part – as showcases for their owner's wealth, good breeding and excellent taste. Laws passed by the shogun said that only samurai families could buy luxury goods. And so a beautiful, well-furnished castle became visible proof of high rank. Screens separated areas where important visitors were received from the 'working' parts of the keep, and were decorated with paintings of plants, birds and flowers in glowing colours and glittering with gold. Rafters overhead were carved and painted, and furnishings – tables, chests, and dishes and bowls for serving food – were exquisitely made from rare woods, lacquer-ware, and fine porcelain. Like the outside of a castle, the inside was designed to impress.

At Nijo castle, one of the finest screen paintings of the samurai period has survived.

It shows pine trees set against a shimmering golden background.

The ceiling above is decorated with birds perching among red and white flowers.

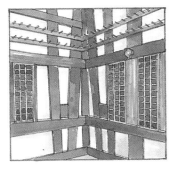

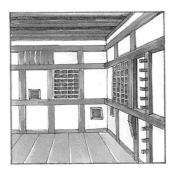

Wells supplied essential drinking water. They were kept carefully guarded. At Himeji castle, there were 10 wells.

Diagonal braces, cut from thick beams of wood, were used to strengthen the corner posts of tall castles.

Inner walls were made out of moveable wood and paper screens. Outer walls had holes for shooting at enemies.

Well-defended doors were essential. This door from Himeji Castle had locks, bolts, and iron armour-plating outside.

Rich homes would prize beautiful, useful objects like these soup bowls and sweet dishes, or this sake (rice-wine) bottle, shaped like an aubergine. All are made of lacquer.

Mats, called tatami, covered castle floors, and were used for sitting and sleeping. They were made of rice-husks sandwiched between two layers of tightly-woven reeds.

The richer you were, the thicker the mats you could afford. Mats in the emperor's palace were almost 50 per cent thicker than in ordinary homes.

Because everyone sat (or knelt) on the floor, tables and chests were low built.

PEOPLE OF THE CASTLE

One historian has calculated that castle-building was the biggest industry in 16th- and 17th-century Japan. Constructing, decorating, repairing and maintaining castles employed a great many people, from the 'bugyo' (high-ranking commissioner of works) to the lowliest labourers.

A large number of people were also needed to keep a castle running from day-to-day. As well as being a fortress, a castle was a home, so servants were employed to cook, clean, mend clothes, care for children, and wait on the samurai family. There might be poets and musicians, to entertain them. The castle was a centre of estate administration, so managers and clerks were busy, inspecting the samurai's farms,

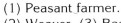

(1) Peasant farmer.
(2) Weaver. (3) Basket-maker. (4) Blacksmith.
(5) Leatherworker.
(6) Porter. (7) Potter.
(8) Swordsmith.
(9) Estate manager.

(10) Builder.
(11) Architect.
(12) Screen-painter.
(13) Widowed grandmother.
(14) Samurai's wife.
(15) Maid. (16) Son and heir. (17) Daughter.

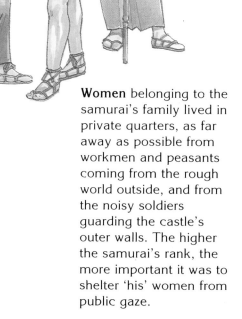

Women belonging to the samurai's family lived in private quarters, as far away as possible from workmen and peasants coming from the rough world outside, and from the noisy soldiers guarding the castle's outer walls. The higher the samurai's rank, the more important it was to shelter 'his' women from public gaze.

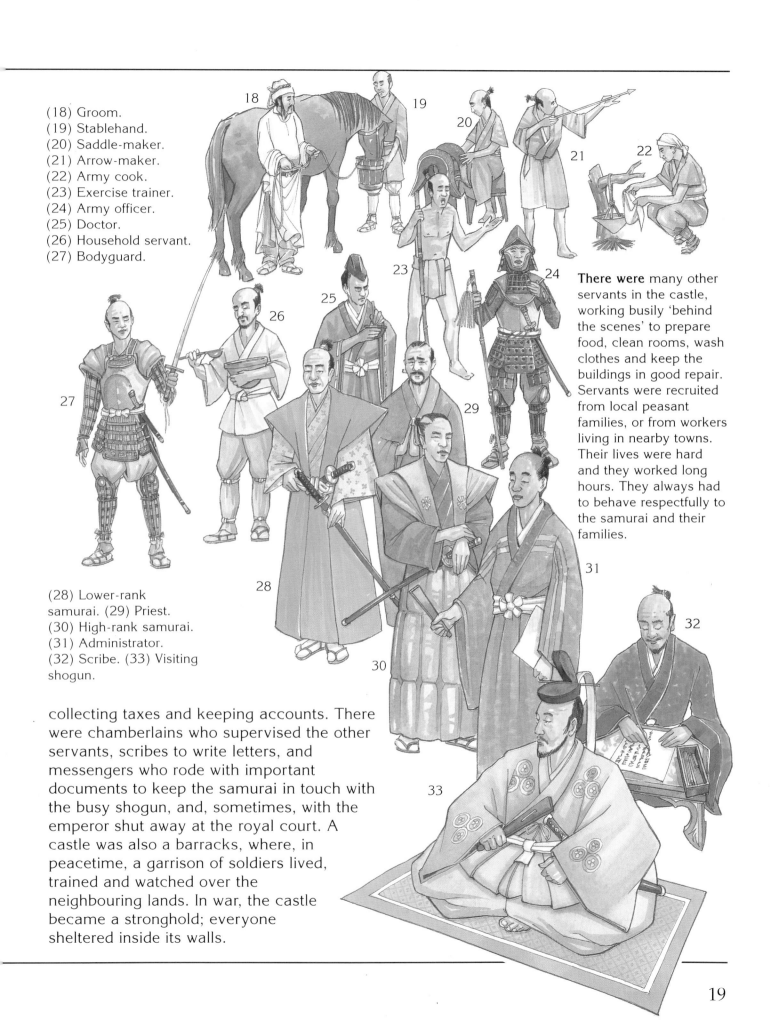

(18) Groom.
(19) Stablehand.
(20) Saddle-maker.
(21) Arrow-maker.
(22) Army cook.
(23) Exercise trainer.
(24) Army officer.
(25) Doctor.
(26) Household servant.
(27) Bodyguard.

There were many other servants in the castle, working busily 'behind the scenes' to prepare food, clean rooms, wash clothes and keep the buildings in good repair. Servants were recruited from local peasant families, or from workers living in nearby towns. Their lives were hard and they worked long hours. They always had to behave respectfully to the samurai and their families.

(28) Lower-rank samurai. (29) Priest. (30) High-rank samurai. (31) Administrator. (32) Scribe. (33) Visiting shogun.

collecting taxes and keeping accounts. There were chamberlains who supervised the other servants, scribes to write letters, and messengers who rode with important documents to keep the samurai in touch with the busy shogun, and, sometimes, with the emperor shut away at the royal court. A castle was also a barracks, where, in peacetime, a garrison of soldiers lived, trained and watched over the neighbouring lands. In war, the castle became a stronghold; everyone sheltered inside its walls.

CASTLES AND TOWNS

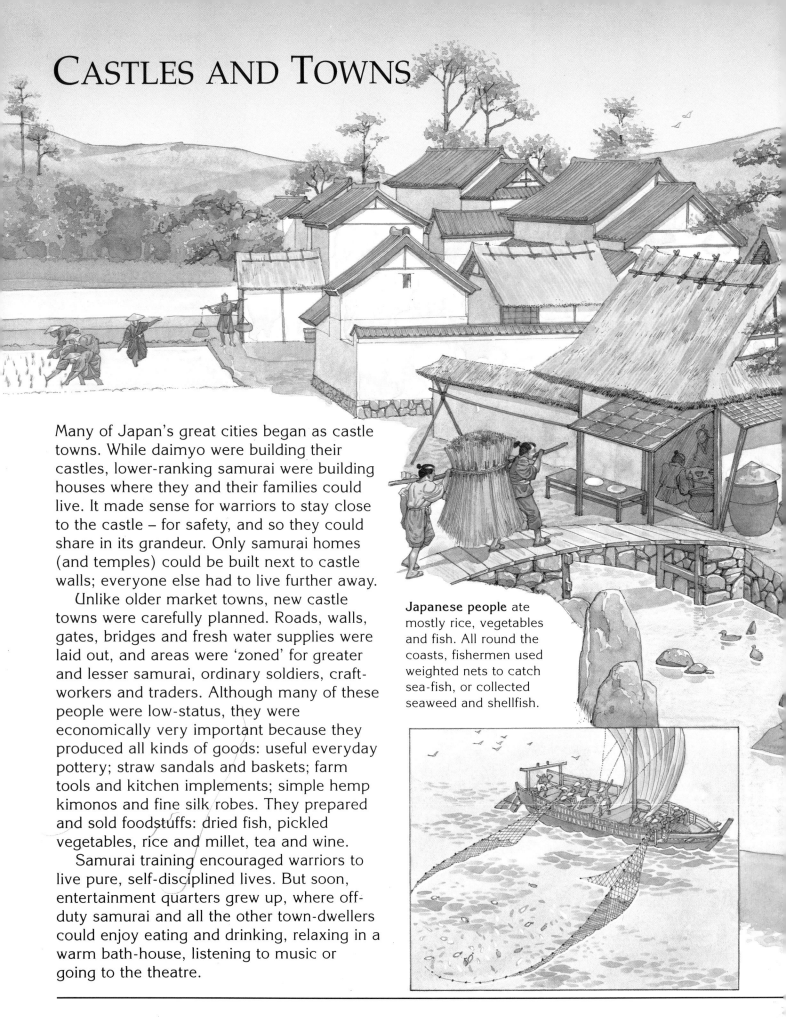

Many of Japan's great cities began as castle towns. While daimyo were building their castles, lower-ranking samurai were building houses where they and their families could live. It made sense for warriors to stay close to the castle – for safety, and so they could share in its grandeur. Only samurai homes (and temples) could be built next to castle walls; everyone else had to live further away.

Unlike older market towns, new castle towns were carefully planned. Roads, walls, gates, bridges and fresh water supplies were laid out, and areas were 'zoned' for greater and lesser samurai, ordinary soldiers, craft-workers and traders. Although many of these people were low-status, they were economically very important because they produced all kinds of goods: useful everyday pottery; straw sandals and baskets; farm tools and kitchen implements; simple hemp kimonos and fine silk robes. They prepared and sold foodstuffs: dried fish, pickled vegetables, rice and millet, tea and wine.

Samurai training encouraged warriors to live pure, self-disciplined lives. But soon, entertainment quarters grew up, where off-duty samurai and all the other town-dwellers could enjoy eating and drinking, relaxing in a warm bath-house, listening to music or going to the theatre.

Japanese people ate mostly rice, vegetables and fish. All round the coasts, fishermen used weighted nets to catch sea-fish, or collected seaweed and shellfish.

ENTERTAINING VISITORS

For top-ranking samurai, entertaining visitors was an important political duty, as well as (sometimes) a pleasure. A daimyo had great power within his own estates - he could make his own laws, raise his own taxes and even invent his own weights and measures. But if he wanted to survive, he also needed to make allies from outside, to help him defend his lands when they were attacked by enemy samurai in times of civil war. Alliances might be made by treaties, through arranged marriages, and by entertaining 'useful' friends. Daimyo Hideyoshi (1536–1598) once gave a tea-party for 5,000 guests.

Formal entertainment like this was not always about having fun. Rather, it was a compliment to the nobility and elegance of your guests. Of course, you offered them fine food and drink – and carefully arranged the seating plan according to their rank, so as not to offend anyone. But you might also invite them to share in traditional noble pastimes, such as cherry-blossom viewing or taking an evening stroll in a beautiful garden to gaze at the full moon. Then, everyone could display their good education and artistic sensitivity by quoting classical poetry and commenting on the scenery.

To entertain a few close friends, you go to a quiet corner of the garden, to admire autumn leaves and tell traditional stories, or play the flute. Or you might invite friends to share the Zen Buddhist-inspired tea ceremony.

Through slow, careful ritual, everyone present was encouraged to share moments of tranquil thought. This strengthened the bonds of friendship. But some samurai thought it made people forget their warrior ideals.

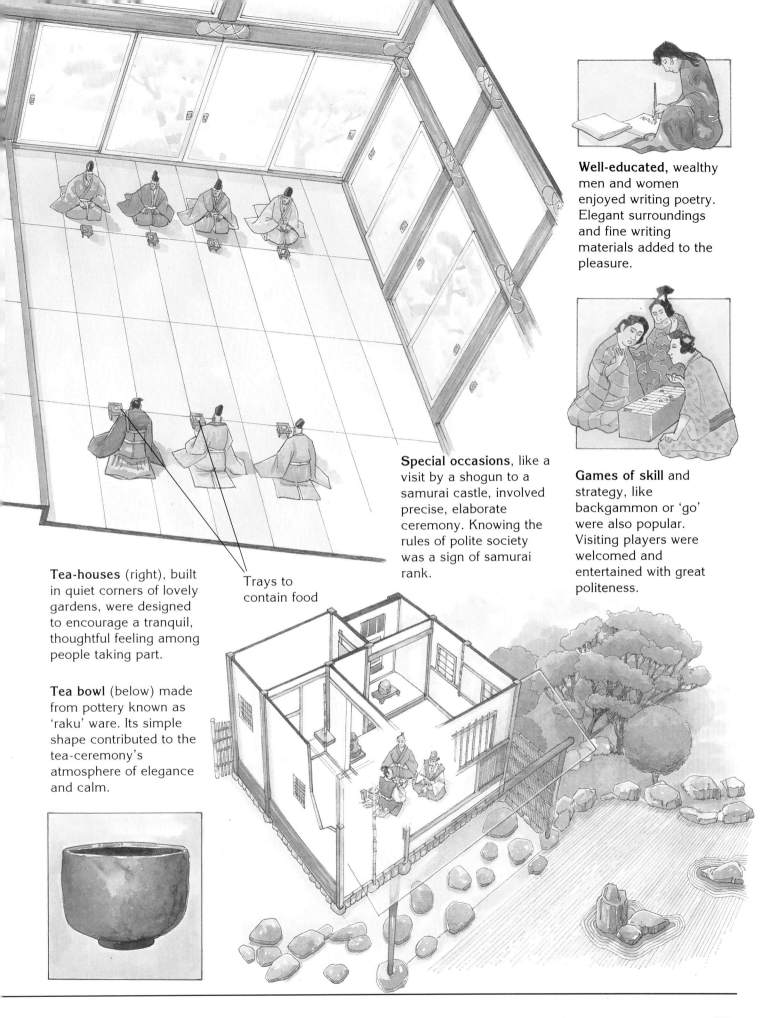

Well-educated, wealthy men and women enjoyed writing poetry. Elegant surroundings and fine writing materials added to the pleasure.

Games of skill and strategy, like backgammon or 'go' were also popular. Visiting players were welcomed and entertained with great politeness.

Special occasions, like a visit by a shogun to a samurai castle, involved precise, elaborate ceremony. Knowing the rules of polite society was a sign of samurai rank.

Trays to contain food

Tea-houses (right), built in quiet corners of lovely gardens, were designed to encourage a tranquil, thoughtful feeling among people taking part.

Tea bowl (below) made from pottery known as 'raku' ware. Its simple shape contributed to the tea-ceremony's atmosphere of elegance and calm.

WOMEN'S LIVES

Traditionally, a woman of the samurai class was brought up to believe that she was inferior to men. It was her duty to serve three masters: her father, her husband and her son. A high-ranking woman had little freedom: marriage was her career; she could not stay single. Her husband was chosen by her parents. Alliances between samurai families were too important to leave to chance.

A wife's first duty was to bear a son to inherit her husband's land. It was also her task to educate her daughters, teaching them suitable manners for polite society, how to read and write, and how to wear elaborate ceremonial clothes.

Samurai women owed their rank – and their safety – to samurai fighting skills.

Some women relied on men to defend them, but others chose to learn martial arts themselves.

Nursemaids cared for young children. They also found time to join in their games, like flying kites.

Old women and widows led quiet lives. They could offer good advice, but most had little power.

Women servants worked at many tasks around the castle: (1) Cleaner. (2) Housemaid – shown here rolling bedding mats. (3) Cook. (4) Ladies' maid.

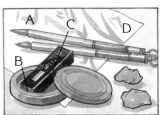

Writing materials: (A) Brush. (B) Ink-stone. (C) Block of solid ink. (D) Rice paper.

The work of samurai wives: (5) commanding soldiers when their husbands were away; (6) doing accounts; (7) giving birth to heirs; (8) offering prayers as Buddhist nuns.

In the towns, women worked as companions (geisha) and as entertainers. Samurai men visited them off- duty, for relaxation. Many women were skilled musicians, poets and storytellers.

Some samurai women became poets and novelists; some won praise for their scholarship, or for their holy lives. They fought bravely and intelligently to defend their homes. Hosokawa Jako (1542-1616) climbed up to the roof of her castle to spy on enemy soldiers below, then sketched a careful plan of their camp with her lip-rouge. Women from lower ranks had much more freedom – though only through necessity. They became servants, farm labourers and shop-keepers, or helped their husbands with their work.

Below:
The Chinese calendar.

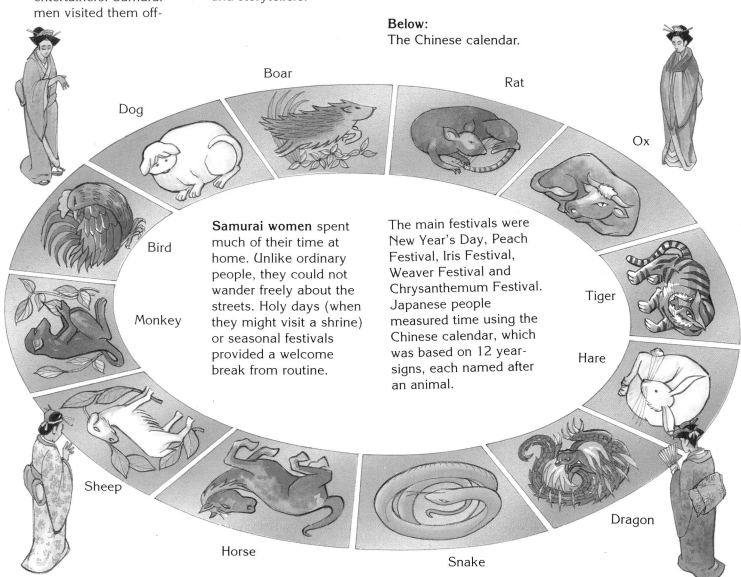

Boar

Dog

Rat

Ox

Bird

Tiger

Monkey

Hare

Samurai women spent much of their time at home. Unlike ordinary people, they could not wander freely about the streets. Holy days (when they might visit a shrine) or seasonal festivals provided a welcome break from routine.

The main festivals were New Year's Day, Peach Festival, Iris Festival, Weaver Festival and Chrysanthemum Festival. Japanese people measured time using the Chinese calendar, which was based on 12 year-signs, each named after an animal.

Sheep

Dragon

Horse

Snake

Becoming a samurai began at birth. You had to be born to samurai parents or be adopted by them.

As a future member of the army, you could not be left-handed. You were trained to use your right.

You were taught to co-operate unselfishly with other boys. At 7 years old, you went to school.

Aged 10, you spent 12 hours a day at school. You learned to fight, as well as school subjects.

SAMURAI TRAINING

Samurai soldiers were young – they could be only 13 or 14. Today, this might seem surprising, but a boy born to a samurai family had been trained for warfare from birth. Like samurai girls, he had no choice; being a warrior was his career.

A samurai boy was taught two basic skills, how to survive and how to kill. Both involved long, sometimes painful training, with wooden weapons to learn defensive swordplay, and real, sharp weapons (thrust into straw mats) when practising the kill. Archery training involved shooting at moving targets (sometimes dogs were used for this).

Your new lifestyle included time off to relax.

With other samurai you drank warm sake and played go.

The Chinese teacher Lanqi Daolong reached Japan in 1246. He brought with him a new form of Buddhism, called 'Zen'. It soon found favour with the shogun and his samurai.

Experienced warriors and new recruits took part in regular training exercises, to make sure they kept fit and well-prepared for battle. One popular form of training was an 'inuomono' (dog-hunt). At other practice sessions, archers mounted on horseback and on foot fired at mock targets fixed in the ground.

You learned about battle techniques and heard stories of past victories from top samurai.

You also learned mental discipline, good manners and respect for older people.

Between 13 and 15, you officially became an adult, after taking part in the 'genbuku' ceremony.

As well as a new, adult, hairstyle (left), you would be given a suit of armour, ready for battle.

You were trained to fight by a senior sword-master. You had to learn to defend yourself on the battlefield. Your class-mates watched your lessons, and it was a disgrace to appear weak or afraid.

After the 16th century, when guns came to Japan, boys were taught to 'load, aim and fire' – which was far quicker and simpler than training with traditional weapons. To survive, a samurai had to think quickly in battle. High-ranking families prided themselves on their disciplined and intellectual approach to war. They taught their sons games like go, believing these would train their minds. Other survival training involved wild horse chases, learning to wrestle wearing armour, and how to fight on horseback. Boys even learned how to tie up prisoners. This was important because if they used the wrong sort of knot, their captives might escape.

ARMS AND ARMOUR

Samurai and ashigaru fought with four main weapons: swords, lances, bows and guns. Bows and arrows had been used in Japan for thousands of years. Bows were long (about 2 metres) and flexible, made of strips of wood and bamboo bound tightly together. There were at least 12 different types of arrow head, mostly made of stone. Some were hollow, and whistled as they flew through the air, causing fear and panic. Others were specially sharp to pierce armour, or barbed, to stick in flesh. Like lances (about 2.5 metres long, and used for stabbing and slashing), bows were carried by ashigaru. The samurai's chosen weapon was a sword. Japanese swordsmiths were so skilful that some swords came to be credited with super-human powers. A few even had names. A great deal of ancient ritual – as well as technical expertise, rolling and folding fine strips of steel – was involved in their production. Swordsmiths prayed, bathed and purified themselves before making a special blade. Guns were unknown before the 16th century. They were copied, with improvements, from Portuguese arquebuses, brought to Japan by merchants in 1542. They used gunpowder, lit by a smouldering cord, to fire metal shot. Guns were effective in battle, but despised by ancient samurai families.

Hand-to-hand combat was a very important skill. Students were trained by the best sword-masters. Jomyo Meishu was a 12th-century warrior monk. He bravely challenged his enemies and no-one dared to fight him single-handed.

A good suit of armour was one of a samurai's most treasured posessions. He relied on it to help save his life. Samurai armour was skilfully made and beautifully decorated. High ranking warriors wore suits of plate armour, made of rigid panels of iron laced or riveted together, sometimes combined with chainmail and tough rawhide. Ashigaru wore thinner, lightweight 'folding armour', made of small metal plates.

For a helmet, up to 32 curved metal panels were riveted together and topped with a crest of painted wood. Flexible nape-guards, made of metal strips, protected the neck. Metal face masks – painted red, for anger – might be added. But they were hot, uncomfortable and made it difficult to see.

M

28

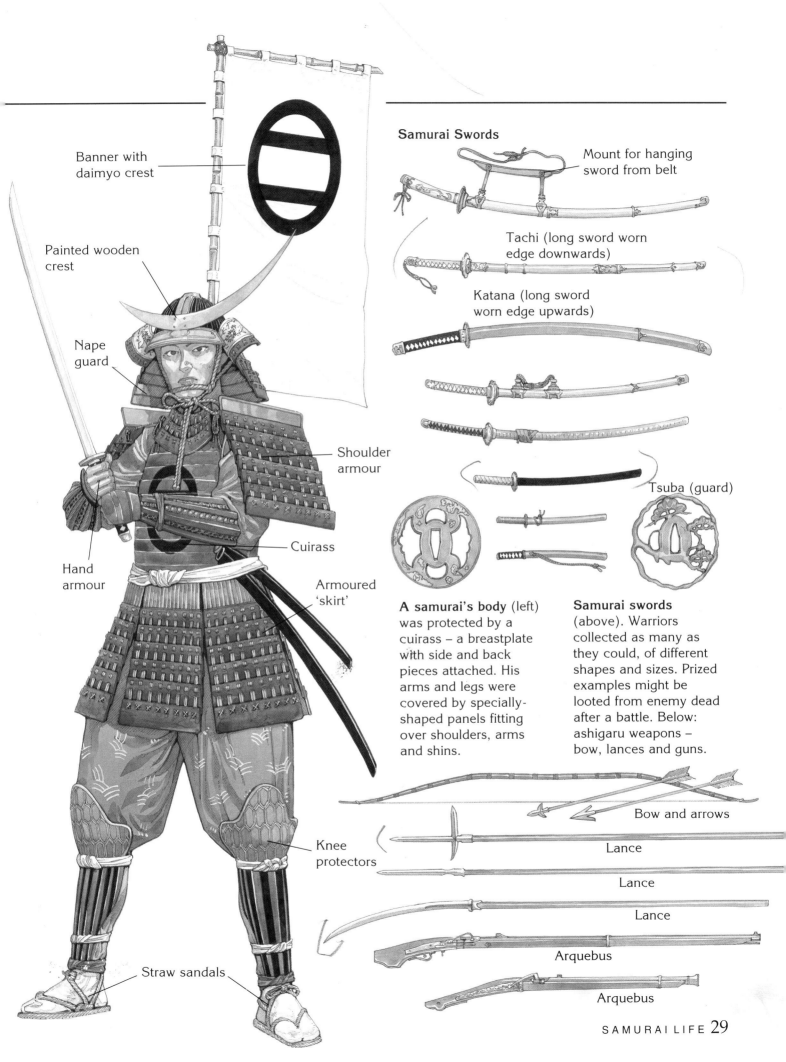

Banner with daimyo crest

Painted wooden crest

Nape guard

Hand armour

Shoulder armour

Cuirass

Armoured 'skirt'

Knee protectors

Straw sandals

Samurai Swords

Mount for hanging sword from belt

Tachi (long sword worn edge downwards)

Katana (long sword worn edge upwards)

Tsuba (guard)

A samurai's body (left) was protected by a cuirass – a breastplate with side and back pieces attached. His arms and legs were covered by specially-shaped panels fitting over shoulders, arms and shins.

Samurai swords (above). Warriors collected as many as they could, of different shapes and sizes. Prized examples might be looted from enemy dead after a battle. Below: ashigaru weapons – bow, lances and guns.

Bow and arrows

Lance

Lance

Lance

Arquebus

Arquebus

A Day in the Life of a Samurai

Takeda Shingen was a famous samurai. His younger brother (we do not know his name) wrote: 'The samurai must never relax his watchfulness. Even when he is alone with his wife, he ought to have his sword by his side.' Shingen's brother did not mean that samurai women were untrustworthy. Rather, he was saying that a samurai must always put his warrior duty first, even before the people he loves.

This was a lofty ideal, and hard to live up to. How far was it followed? For many lower-ranking samurai, in peacetime, life must have seemed pleasantly routine. There was battle-training, guard duty and regular

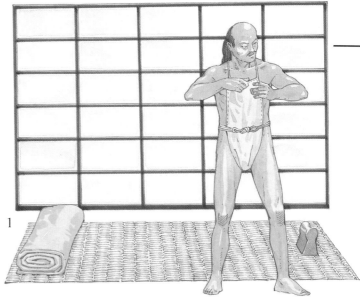

7 am (dawn) Gets up, gets dressed, ties hair in topknot. Rolls bedding mat neatly away.

9 am On lookout duty. With other low-rank samurai, he patrols the top of the castle walls.

7.30 am Has breakfast with his wife and children: rice and pickled vegetables.

8 am Makes his way through the town streets from his family's lodgings to the castle.

1 pm After lunch, time for fitness training. Practises sword fighting with expert teacher.

3 pm Leaves castle to go and visit local craftsman, who is mending some of his armour.

5 pm Now he is clean and purified, he can visit the Buddhist temple nearby to pray.

4 pm Washes off sweat and dirt in open-air bath at rocky pool filled by natural hot springs.

8 pm Dinner-break in the castle hall along with other samurai: they eat fish, soup and rice.

11 pm It's time to go home. His wife greets him and tells him what she and the children have done all day.

12 midnight Bedtime. But before sleep, time to sit quietly and meditate. How well he has performed his tasks as a samurai?

10 pm Guard-duty over, calls in to have a drink of rice wine with samurai friends in town.

patrols, plus the comforts of home life at the end of the day. In wartime, everything was different. A samurai had to follow his daimyo 'lord' into battle. He would spend weeks, perhaps months, living rough in wild country. He faced enemy ambushes, disease and exhaustion, and the chances were that, sooner or later, he would be killed. We do not know exactly what proportion of samurai survived to a ripe old age, but the casualty figures for most samurai battles were horrendous.

New Samurai Style

Traditionally, samurai believed that too great an interest in the arts (and in traditional religion and philosophy) would make you 'soft'. Craft skills, except sword-making and calligraphy, were lower-class. A warrior should naturally take care to buy the best armour, and proudly wear a surcoat with his family crest, but otherwise, brightly-coloured clothes and furnishings were for actors and women.

But in 1576, samurai Oda Nobunaga seized control of Japan. He burned ancient Buddhist temples, because some rich and powerful priests were a threat to his rule.

Decorative techniques

To make fine spray: balance wet paintbrush across wrist and flick sharply.

To apply gold leaf:
(1) Beat gold wire until it flattens and spreads into little flakes.

(2) Rub dry paintbrush in hair. It will become charged with static electricity.

(3) Hold charged paintbrush over flakes of gold leaf. They will 'jump' onto the brush.

(4) Hold brush over painting. Tap handle; gold flakes will drop off and stick to painting.

Above:
Patterned silk kimono, 17th century.

Sliding doors (right) with a coloured ink drawing of a crane (a bird, symbol of long life) and pine trees. Painted by Kano Eitoku, 1566.

Then he began to build a castle at Azuchi; it was completed in 1579. To decorate it, Nobunaga employed Japan's best painters. Long years of civil war were coming to an end, and samurai began to have time and money to spend on other things than war. As we have seen, they soon copied Nobunaga's ideas, and a new, samurai style – bold, bright and using luxurious materials – became popular. It was copied for male and female clothing, especially for loose robes called kosode or kimono, and for weapons and armour, too. Formal clothes, for the shogun's or emperor's court, were still traditionally simple and dark coloured.

Above:
A decorated lacquer box. Left: A samurai saddle made of leather and wood.

Elaborate armour (right), made in 1859, at the end of the samurai period. It is constructed of gold-lacquered iron and leather segments, held together with silk thread. The sleeves and legs are chain-mail, and the boots are made of fur. The helmet has an iron mask, decorated with animal hair.

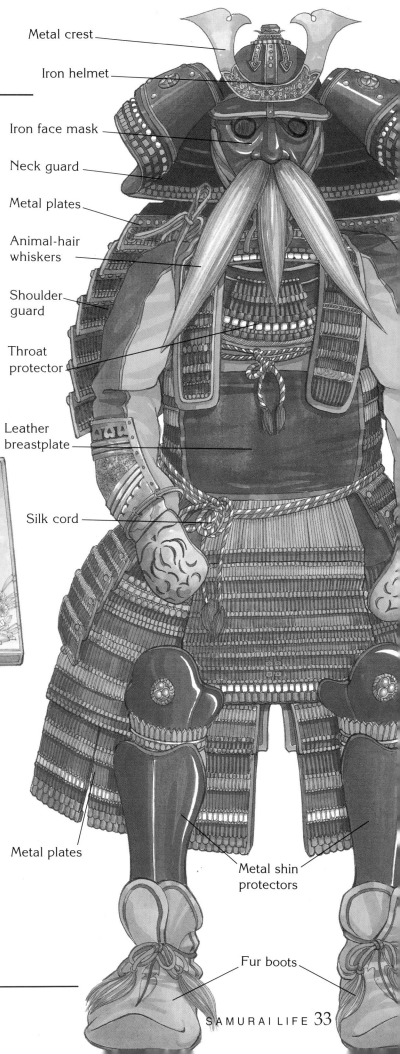

Metal crest
Iron helmet
Iron face mask
Neck guard
Metal plates
Animal-hair whiskers
Shoulder guard
Throat protector
Leather breastplate
Silk cord
Metal plates
Metal shin protectors
Fur boots

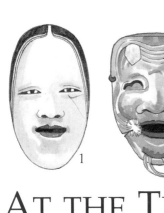
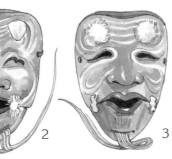

1 2 3 4 5 6

AT THE THEATRE

When shogun Tokugawa Ieyasu invited a group of high-ranking samurai to dinner at his castle in 1603, he arranged for a Noh play to be performed to entertain them. Like many samurai, he had a specially-built Noh stage, close to the large hall where he received visitors.

This Noh performance was appreciated by its audience. But what was it like? Noh plays were ancient and traditional. The book telling Noh actors how to perform was written in 1400; its instructions were followed for centuries. Noh actors – all men – did not try to appear true to life.

Masks worn by actors in Noh plays: (1) Calm young woman. (2) Joyful old man. (3) Kindly old man. (4) Woman betrayed by her lover. (5) Deserted woman driven mad by jealousy. (6) Angry warrior.

Noh actors changed and made-up in the dressing room, then sat in the 'mirror room' to meditate and prepare their minds for the coming performance.

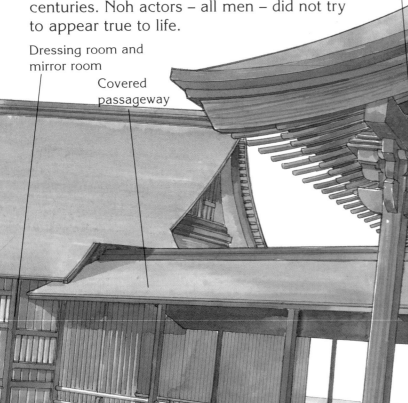

Dressing room and mirror room

Covered passageway

Main stage

Painted screen

A   B   C   D   E   F   G

Kabuki actors had to be versatile. The Japanese artist Utagawa Toyokuni, who lived in the 18th century, drew this series of costume to show all the different kinds of parts an actor might have to play during his career: (A) Daiymo. (B) Shogun. (C) Town-dweller. (D) Low-ranking samurai. (E) Army commander. (F) Master swordsman. (G) Woman.

Instead, in some ways, they resembled samurai themselves: powerful, well-trained, disciplined and formal. Actors wore masks and heavy costumes; the spirit of each mask was meant to inspire them. On stage, they used stiff, stylised gestures to tell the audience what was happening. For example, gently moving a sleeve meant 'I am falling in love'. Music and dance sustained the dramatic mood. Another type of drama, Kabuki, was performed in castle towns from the 17th century. It was a complete contrast to Noh plays, being action-packed, loud with songs and speeches, full of dramatic fights, brave heroines and dastardly villains. Some shoguns tried to ban Kabuki, but it was too popular.

Traditionally, Noh theatres had a square stage with space for the orchestra behind. The audience sat in an open-air stand.

The first Noh plays were performed at shrines, often in front of sacred trees. So the screen at the back of each Noh stage was painted with an old pine tree, as a reminder of Noh drama's religious origins.

Side stage for chorus

By the 18th century, wealthy spectators at Kabuki plays were sheltered by tiled roofs. Some also paid for private boxes, screened by bamboo blinds, where they could meet friends – or even lovers. The shoguns did not approve.

A WARLORD AND HIS ARMY

Like the rest of Japanese society, samurai armies were strictly ordered by rank. Commanders came from the samurai class. They were expected to arrive for battle with a pre-arranged number of fully equipped fighting men. The size of each private army depended on how much land a samurai had. His wealth was measured in 'koku' – the amount of rice needed to feed one man for a year. A commander was expected to provide six soldiers per 100 koku. We can judge the vastness of some samurai estates by the size of their armies: for example, in 1587, the Shimazu family attacked Minamata castle with around 100,000 soldiers – equivalent to over a million koku of land. Armies were divided into separate camps, each led by a senior samurai and staffed by officers (who

On the march, armies slept where they could (officers in temples or farmhouses, ordinary soldiers in barns or under bushes). When the battle site was reached, they pitched tents inside a circle of 'tobari' (camp-curtains) – proud banners displaying the daimyo's crest.

Samurai fighting skills:
(A) Archer.
(B) Arquebusier (a type of gun). (C) Spearman.
(D) Flag-bearer.
(E) Army commander.
(F) Bodyguard.
(G) Footsoldier.

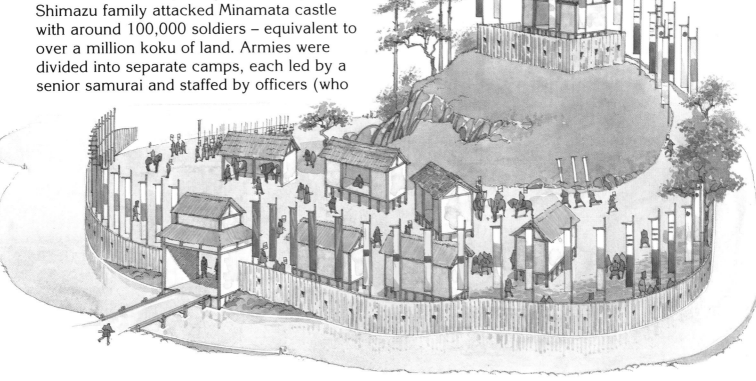

Dressing for battle:
(1) Put on loincloth.
(2) Then short kimono.
(3) Tie baggy trousers around waist.

(4) Fasten shin-pads.
(5) Fix thigh-guards.
(6) Pull on chain-mail sleeves. (7) Add chest-guard.

(8) Now buckle on body-armour (breast-plate, back plate and skirt). Hold in place with silk cord.

(9) Cover hair with scarf of soft cloth. (10) Tie on helmet. Arrange shoulder-guards and face mask.

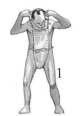        

A   B   C   D   E   F   G

organised the fighting), banner-carriers, cooks, baggage-handlers, straw sandal-carriers, grooms (for the war-horses) and porters to carry arrows and gunpowder. The commander's personal staff included guards for his treasure-chest, hat-carriers and pages. There were signallers (who sent messages with drums and gongs) and doctors. They only treated senior men, so ordinary soldiers relied on folk-remedies such as eating horse-dung to stop bleeding, or bathing wounds in your own heated urine to ease pain.

Victorious troops rode back to camp carrying the heads of enemies they had killed in battle. It was more honourable for defeated soldiers to be killed – even like this – than to survive.

ON PATROL

Even in peacetime, a samurai soldier spent some of his time out on patrol, defending estate boundaries. In wartime, armies advanced on foot, surviving as best they could in hostile lands. In dangerous situations, they might rely on knowledge learned from books on warfare. For example, the oldest and best book, 'The Art of War', written by Chinese general Sun Tzu between 450 and 421 BC, advised: 'Birds rising in flight ahead is a sign that the enemy is waiting to ambush you.'

Life on patrol might be exciting, but it was hard and tiring, too. Soldiers had to carry everything they needed, and wore their heavy armour all the time. It soon became smelly and infested with fleas and lice – killed by 'smoking' armour over a hot fire. Essential supplies included spare weapons and (for guns) matches and gunpowder, strong thread for repairing armour, fresh straw sandals and a change of underwear, plus a straw mat for a bed. Food was mostly 'instant' rice, cooked and dried before setting out. On patrol it could be reconstituted by adding hot water – boiled in a metal helmet. It might be flavoured with dried tuna, which was light and easy to carry, but soldiers also tried to catch traditional 'stamina foods': rabbit and wild deer.

In wartime, everything needed by a samurai army had to be light and easy to carry. As well as food, weapons and armour, soldiers also carried a portable Buddhist shrine, which could be set up in the army camp and used to provide a place for worhip and meditation. Samurai believed these helped them to fight better.

掠疾
如如
火風

Long, narrow flags, called nobori, were carried into battle. Each flag was decorated with a daimyo's crest. If soldiers became scattered on the battlefield, the flags helped them find their way back to their comrades again.

Originally, the flags were fastened just to the top of a 'T'-shaped wooden pole. But after around 1500, each flag was laced down one side as well. This stopped them flapping, and made the crests easier to read at a distance.

Flags were often carried by ashigaru (ordinary soldiers). Each samurai army had dozens of flag-bearers. Carrying a flag was risky – bearers had to stay close to the army commanders, sometimes right in the heart of the battle. The flag was fixed to each bearer's back. This left both his hands free for fighting, but also made him a conspicuous target for arrows.

CASTLE UNDER SIEGE

The architects who designed samurai castles called their ground-plans 'nawabari', which means 'stretched cord'. This was how they laid out the arrangement of moats, earthworks and stone walls that defended every castle keep. These outer barriers were essential to protect a castle from enemy attack. The ideal number was three, but the layout at each castle varied, according to the site. Barriers stopped besieging armies getting close enough to attack defenders sheltering inside the wood and plaster keep. A skilled bowman could shoot an arrow 380 metres; an arquebus could kill at almost 500 metres.

Water-filled moats were a useful way of defending a castle. They stopped outer walls being undermined and made it easy to shoot at enemies trying to sail across in boats. But water could be used to attack castles, too. In 1538, the samurai Toyotomi Hideyoshi ordered his troops to build a dam across a river close to Kameyama castle, which he was besieging. As the flood waters rose the castle's defenders surrendered.

If an army breached the outer defences, the keep was almost certain to be destroyed. Fire was the greatest hazard – the keep's wooden frame was highly inflammable. Many samurai castles burned down only a few years after they were built. But even if the outer defences held, a besieged castle's inhabitants might face slow death from starvation or disease unless allies arrived to attack the besiegers from the rear. On the greatest samurai estates, minor castles were built all around the boundaries as a first line of defence and as barracks for 'rescue' troops.

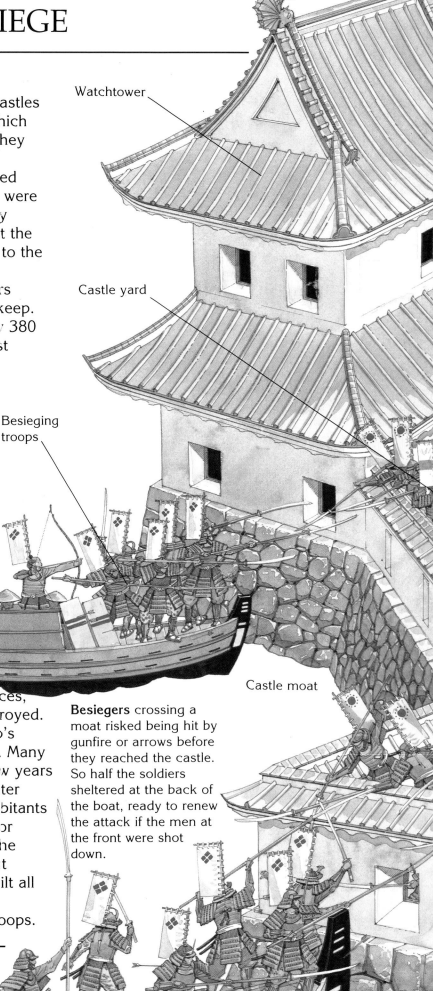

Watchtower

Castle yard

Besieging troops

Castle moat

Besiegers crossing a moat risked being hit by gunfire or arrows before they reached the castle. So half the soldiers sheltered at the back of the boat, ready to renew the attack if the men at the front were shot down.

Slit window protects
archer but allows
arrows to be fired

THE END OF THE SAMURAI

After 1603, the Tokugawa shoguns ruled Japan. Gradually, all the warlike samurai families were 'tamed' by Tokugawa power. After 1649, daimyo status depended not on fame and good fortune in war, but on the number of soldiers a samurai could provide for national defence. It was as if samurai had become state servants, no longer the proud, independent warriors of old.

At the same time, the Tokugawa shoguns introduced two strict new policies: peace at home and isolation from abroad. There was now no need for samurai fighting skills. Samurai kept their rank, their traditions and their estates, but were increasingly useless. Even their wealth dwindled, as towns flourished, and low- ranking merchants, craft-workers and entertainers grew rich.

In 1868, there was a revolution. The Tokugawa shoguns were deposed and the imperial system was restored after more than 250 years. Emperor Meiji rapidly introduced a policy of westernisation, and samurai traditions seemed even more useless than before. But they were not. To many Japanese – and to people in other lands – the old samurai ideals of honour, bravery, loyalty and self-sacrifice remained a noble inspiration.

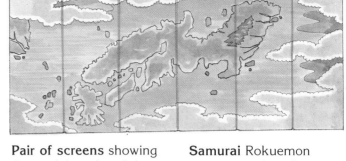

Pair of screens showing Japan (above) and the rest of the world (below) by a Japanese artist of the Edo period (1632-1868).

Samurai Rokuemon Tsunenaga (right) led a Japanese trading voyage to America and Europe in 1613, but the project failed.

During the 17th and 18th centuries, when Japan was closed to foreigners, Japanese ships like this left Nagasaki to trade with the outside world.

Nagasaki, with its splendid natural harbour, was Japan's main port. This is how it was pictured on a late 17th-century map.

Commodore Matthew Perry, commander of the fleet of American 'black ships' (warships) that reached Japan in 1853.

Right:
Image or reality? Rich costume and warlike make-up for an actor playing the part of a samurai in the Kabuki play 'Shibaraku'. But by the 19th century, few samurai were wealthy, and fewer still were skilled warriors.

The western-style Mitsui building in Tokyo. It was built in 1872 for a company founded by a samurai-turned-merchant.

Continuing tradition. Picture of a pilot with a samurai sword from a Japanese wartime magazine, 1939-1945.

As well as providing good physical training, Japanese martial arts also aim to encourage self-discipline and high moral standards.

Japanese martial arts, like Kendo (The Way of the Sword, right) Judo ('The Way of Gentleness') and Karate ('The Empty Hand Way', above) have become popular sports in many countries.

SOME FAMOUS SAMURAI

Prince Yamato – The First Samurai

Prince Yamato is said to have lived about 100 BC, and to have been the son of Emperor Keiko. Many stories were told of his brave adventures. He was fearless (he fought and defeated many of the emperor's enemies), ruthless (he killed his brother for turning up late to a meal) and cunning (he disguised himself as an old woman to get inside a rebel's castle). He received help from the gods – his aunt was high priestess of the sun goddess. He owned a magic sword, made from a serpent's tail. He was the best fighter of his age.

But, sadly, Yamato may never have existed. Like many legendary figures, his story is probably a mixture of several real warriors' adventures, mixed with ancient religious beliefs.

The Soga Revolution

The Soga family were rich, noble warriors with friends – and enemies – at the emperor's court. They wanted to 'modernise' the way Japan was governed by introducing new ideas borrowed from China. But other noble families disagreed. So, in 587, Soga warriors fought a battle at Shigisen, and won. In 592, one of the family, Prince Shotoku, became emperor. He passed many new laws, transforming the way the country was run.

Fujiwara: Samurai Wives and Mothers

Soga rule did not last long. In 645 another warrior family – the Fujiwara – became even more powerful at court. They did not become emperors, but for the next 1,200 years, Fujiwara women played a very important role. They married emperors and gave birth to heirs to the throne. Between 724 and 1900, 54 of the 76 Japanese emperors were the sons of Fujiwara mothers.

Otomo Yakamochi – The First Shogun

Otomo Yakamochi lived in the 8th century (he died in 786). He was not a very effective warrior. In fact, the Emperor Kammu called him an 'incompetent coward'. But he is remembered as being the first warrior to receive the title of shogun.

Minamoto Tametomo – The Greatest Archer

Minamoto Tametomo lived in the 12th century. By the time he was 17, he had become famous for his skill with his bow and arrows. A contemporary chronicle reported that he fought over 20 battles in under two years, and captured dozens of castles. But this may have been exaggerated. The same reporter also claimed that Tametomo's bow-arm was 10 centimetres longer than his other arm. In 1170, Tametomo won even more fame by being the first samurai to commit ritual suicide (called 'seppuku'), rather than face defeat. In later centuries, many samurai followed his example.

Tomoe Gozen

Warrior Lady Tomoe Gozen was the wife of a powerful samurai, Minamoto Yoshinaka. She also took part in the Battle of Uji (in 1180), fighting alongside her husband. Bravely, she tried to fight off the enemy soldiers while he attempted to commit suicide – more honourable than facing defeat. Gozen did not die in the battle, but retired to a Buddhist monastery, and became a nun.

The End of the Taira

The Taira family were the most powerful samurai in 12th-century Japan; they ruled on behalf of the 8-year-old emperor Antoku. But they were defeated at the sea-battle of Dan-no-ura in 1185. They had no choice but mass suicide. Led by Antoku's grandmother, carrying him in her arms, all the leading Taira warriors jumped overboard in their armour, and drowned.

Minamoto Yoritomo – First Shogun for Life

Minamoto Yoritomo won the Gempei War. After many daring – but cruel and ruthless – struggles against the other samurai family who had helped defeat the Taira, he now controlled the country – and the emperor too. In 1192, the old emperor died and a new emperor – Go-Toba – came to the throne. He was only 13. He knew he had to remain friends with Yoritomo. That was the only chance he had of keeping the throne, and ensuring peace for his country. So he made him shogun for life, with the right to pass on the title – and its powers – to his sons.

Kusunoki Masahige – The Loyal Samurai

Most samurai were loyal only to their own families. But Kusunoki Masahige became famous for the support he gave Emperor Go-Daigo, who came to power in 1318. Go-Daigo was one of the few Japanese emperors who wanted – or was able – to stand up to the shoguns and rule for himself. Kusunoki Masahige gave the emperor wise advice, but he was overruled by courtiers, who had none of his samurai skills. However he chose loyally to obey the emperor's orders, and was killed in battle.

Oda Nobunaga – Warlord and Diplomat

Nobunaga (1534-82) came from a low-ranking samurai family, but was so skilful as an army commander that he soon became rich and famous. He fought many battles, but he also sought power through diplomacy and marriage alliances. He encouraged Christian missionaries because he thought they would weaken the power of warlike Buddhist monks. He built a huge, glamorous castle, Azuchi, on a 183-metre cliff on the shores of a lake. He hoped it would be the base from which he could rule all Japan, but soon afterwards, he died in a temple fire that was started deliberately.

Toyotomi Hideyoshi – The Last Great Samurai?

Toyotomi Hideyoshi continued Nobunaga's attempts to unite the warring samurai under a single strong ruler, and, through great skill and bravery in battle, he succeeded. He defeated the last of his rivals in 1590. He also tried to take all weapons away from peasants and farmers, in case they rebelled. He built a magnificent castle at Osaka, and led a (disastrous) invasion of Korea. He was never made shogun; his family were too low-ranking. But for many years until his death in 1598, he was the most powerful man in Japan.

After his death, Hideyoshi was betrayed by his friend the samurai Tokugawa Ieyasu, who had promised to act as guardian for Hideyoshi's young son. Instead, in 1603, Ieyasu seized power for himself, and founded a dynasty of shoguns that ruled for over 250 years.

GLOSSARY

Arquebus, early form of shotgun. It used gunpowder to fire small metal shot.

Ashigaru, ordinary soldier in a samurai army. Not of samurai rank.

Barbed, armed with spikes.

Bath-house, place where men went to relax by bathing – often communally – in large tubs of warm water, sometimes heated by natural springs. Food, drink, music and other entertainments were also available.

Buddhist, follower of the religious teachings of the Indian philosopher-king Gautama Siddhartha (6th century BC), later known as Buddha. Buddhists aimed to live pure, honest, simple lives, trying to follow the 'right path' that would lead them to God. Many Japanese people were Buddhists; others followed the ancient Shinto religion (see below). Today most people Japanese people follow both religions.

Bugyo, overseer or commissioner, in charge of castle building operations.

Burdock piling, way of building walls with large boulders. Burdock is a plant with large round leaves.

Calligraphy, beautiful writing, a prized samurai art.

Chamberlain, senior servant, in charge of running a castle household.

Classical, traditional and respected.

Conspicuous, clearly visible.

Daimyo, lord. Title given to top-ranking, wealthy, powerful samurai who owned castles and great estates.

Disordered piling, way of building walls using small, rough stones packed together.

Gables, pointed roof-ends. Elaborate roofs on Japanese castles were a sign of rank and high status.

Geisha, professional women entertainers who provided companionship for men.

Go, ancient game for two players, rather like the modern game 'Othello'. Black and white stones are placed on a board with the aim of surrounding the largest area.

Hemp, plant with tough fibres that could be woven into coarse cloth.

Husk, outer, papery covering of rice and other grains.

Innovative, full of new ideas.

Intellectual, concerned with thoughts and ideas.

Inuomono, dog-hunt, an army training exercise.

Judo, Japanese martial art. (The 'Way of Gentleness'.)

Kabuki, lively, popular Japanese drama.

Karate, Japanese martial art. (The 'Empty Hand Way' – no weapons are used.)

Kendo, Japanese martial art. (The 'Way of the Sword.)

Kimono, Japanese garment with wrap-over front and wide sleeves.

Koku, a measure of wealth. The amount of rice needed to feed one man for a year.

Lacquer, a precious substance used to decorate fine objects or buildings. It comes from the sap of a Far Eastern tree.

Lance, long-handled weapon, like a spear.

Lip rouge, cosmetic, rather like lipstick.

Nawabari, 'stretched cord', the method, using rope and pegs, of marking a castle's layout on the ground.

Nobori, flag or banner, carried on soldier's backs.

Noh, ancient, upper-class drama.

Pavilions, small, elegant buildings, usually in gardens.

Prefabricated, ready made, in sections that can be assembled later.

Ritual, precise, elaborate ceremony, often with a religious or political meaning.

Samurai, warrior, member of the Japanese upper class. Most powerful from the 12th to the 17th centuries.

Shinto, the ancient, traditional religion of Japan. It is based on reverence for nature-spirits.

Shogun, title of the military ruler of Japan between the 12th and 19th centuries.

Superhuman, with magical, more-than-human powers.

Surcoat, loose robe, worn over armour.

Tatami, floor mats. Used for sitting and sleeping.

Tenshu, strong central tower (keep) of a castle.

Tobari, 'camp-curtains', banners surrounding an army camp.

Tranquil, peaceful and undisturbed.

Zen, branch of the Buddhist religion, popular in Japan, especially among samurai. It stressed mental discipline and self-control.

Zoned, divided into regions (zones), each with a different purpose.

 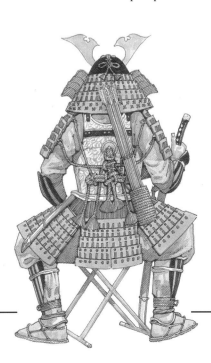

INDEX